JOURNEYS

For kindly strangers encountered on my
own journeys, from Montenegro to Mongolia.

~ *J.L.*

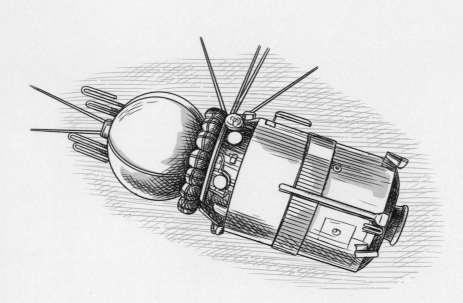

360 DEGREES, an imprint of Tiger Tales

5 River Road, Suite 128, Wilton, CT 06897

Published in the United States 2018

Originally published in Great Britain 2018

by Caterpillar Books

Text by Jonathan Litton

Text copyright © 2018 Caterpillar Books

Illustrated by Chris Chalik, Dave Shephard, Jon Davis, and Leo Hartas

Illustrations copyright © 2018 Caterpillar Books

ISBN-13: 978-1-944530-13-6

ISBN-10: 1-944530-13-4

Printed in China

CPB/1800/0662/0917

For more insight and activities, visit us at www.tigertalesbooks.com

JOURNEYS

by

JONATHAN LITTON

Illustrated by

CHRIS CHALIK

DAVE SHEPHARD

JON DAVIS

LEO HARTAS

HUMAN JOURNEYS

Journeys are in our genes—it seems humans have been programmed to be a traveling species, wandering and wondering our way around the planet. Of course, in the days of hunting and gathering, it was necessary to undertake daily journeys for food. Then, about 200,000 years ago, man began his voyages out of Africa and through the subsequent centuries colonized almost all corners of the globe by foot and on ocean-going craft.

They say that man "settled" when he built farms, villages, towns, and cities, but the wanderlust was never cured. People from all nations and generations have had the urge to travel, and our great explorers and voyagers have come from every culture on Earth.

From Aboriginals who walk through the outback using songs as maps, to Polynesians who made an empire of islands, from Mongolians who saw the world on horseback to an African named Hannibal who sat atop an elephant, different modes of transportation have been chosen according to the terrain in question.

In more modern times, the poles have been magnets to daring explorers, as have the mountaintops, and then the sky became the limit—could man fly? How far? And what about space travel? The limits are defined not by technology but by people's imagination—if people dare to dream it, then more often than not some brave voyager has fulfilled that dream. This is a book of dreamers and doers, and of the wonderful stories they have brought back from faraway lands.

CONTENTS

"If I find land, I will come back and tell you."
—Leif Eriksson

WATER

Traveling through water carries danger—storms, shipwrecks, sharks, and pirates, for starters. But the rewards can be enormous—huge distances can be covered, and the sight of land can reveal food, shelter, metals, new homes, cities, countries, and exotic goods. Humans have been boatbuilders since prehistoric times, and whether they've traveled by canoe, longship, sailing boat, rowboat, or steamship, there has always been an unpredictability and excitement about journeys across water.

MASTERS
of the
SEAS

Long, long ago, Polynesians explored and settled on tiny islands scattered across the Pacific Ocean. They had limited technology and left no written record so dates are uncertain, but historians have pieced together their stories from archaeological evidence and knowledge of the Pacific cultures.

Area settled
by Polynesians

A WORLD OF ISLANDS

It is incredible that Polynesians found tiny specks of land in such a vast area of ocean. They used outrigger canoes with large sails, and navigated using the Sun, Moon, and stars. They also used wildlife to help them—seabirds behave differently around land, as do fish, whales, and dolphins.

Although they didn't write, the Polynesians did weave fantastical maps from coconut trees, which showed islands and ocean currents.

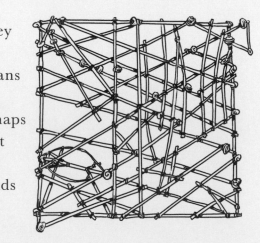

SUPERSTAR OF THE SEAS

Ui-te-Rangiora from the 7th century is said to have ventured south beyond New Zealand and into waters where he saw "rocks grew out of the sea" as well as "a foggy, misty, and dark place not seen by the Sun." Could he have been the first Antarctic explorer?

VOYAGES NORTH

Ancient travels have a degree of mystery—with no surviving written sources from the travelers themselves, how much is fact and how much fiction? What we do know about these two travelers to the far north is that their tales fit in with modern geographical understanding and that their legend lives on.

PYTHEAS THE GREEK AND THE LAND OF THULE

Pytheas was a Greek navigator born in France in about 350 BC. He heard of a land to the north where tin was available, and decided to see for himself. This land was Cornwall in southern Britain, and Pytheas sailed all around the coast of Britain, taking measurements. However, an error meant that he got the shape of Scotland very wrong! Locals told tales of a land even further north called Thule, and again Pytheas set off, finding a land where the Sun hardly set and the seas became icy. Could this have been Iceland?

ST. BRENDAN AND THE ISLE OF SHEEP

Another explorer of the northern waters was an Irish monk named Brendan. In the 6th century AD, he and a small crew set off in search of the Garden of Eden. Along the way he ran into a giant sea monster that spouted water—surely a description of a giant whale. He landed on a place called the Isle of Sheep, which we assume was one of the Faroe Islands, as their present-day name means Isles of Sheep in the local language. No trees grew on the island, so it was the opposite of the Garden of Eden—but it did make for a fantastic travel story, which has been retold for 1,500 years. Brendan even became the patron saint of whales and dolphins!

Faroese coat of arms

"Fear not, brothers, for our God will be unto us a helper, a mariner, and a pilot."

—*St. Brendan*

VOYAGES SOUTH

Beyond the Pillars of Hercules—rocks that protected the western entrance to the Mediterranean—lay the great unknown. Only the bravest navigators dared to point their ships southward and explore the African coast.

HANNO THE NAVIGATOR

Hanno from Carthage (now in Tunisia) became a legend in his own time (about 500 BC). He sailed down the African coast, forming new towns and cities, and told of encounters with natives and gorillas. He survived an erupting volcano and slept on a mysterious island. Although his written work was only 18 lines long, it provided one of the few written records of the region for almost 2,000 years.

SATASPES

Sataspes found himself sentenced to death for kidnapping, but his mother begged for a different punishment—that he must sail all around Africa. Sataspes set off from his native Persia (Iran) and was given ships and a crew in Egypt. He sailed through the Mediterranean and past the great Pillars of Hercules before rounding the western cape of Africa and heading south. After several months, Sataspes reported seeing dwarves who made their clothes from palm leaves. Could these be the pygmy people who continue to live in the forests of West Africa today? Sataspes was forced to turn back, and sadly, he was killed when he returned because he had failed to complete the voyage.

MIDDLE EAST

AFRICA

"There I saw dwarves, who made their clothes from palm leaves."

—SATASPES

VOYAGES EAST

Around 200 BC, the first emperor of China sought the secret of eternal life. A brave navigator went on a voyage lasting 11 years, before reporting that a giant sea monster had blocked his path and that he needed China's best archers to defeat it.

AN UNUSUAL ISLAND

Many Chinese believed that an island existed in the eastern seas that held the secret to eternal youth. It was the meeting point of the immortals—those who never died—and it was believed that visitors to this place could bring back the secret of eternal life. However, the island was covered in clouds and could temporarily hide below water to prevent people from finding it.

THE FIRST VOYAGE

Emperor Qin Shi Huang ("chin shee hwang") called on his people to find this island. An expert navigator named Xu Fu ("shoo foo") was chosen to lead the expedition, and up to 3,000 people were sent with him so that they, too, could benefit from the secrets of everlasting life. In a fleet of bamboo sailing boats, Xu Fu used the stars to guide them.

THE SECOND AND THIRD VOYAGES

After several years, he returned to China with a story of a dragon that told him to bring more people before he would give them the magical herbs. The emperor agreed, and off Xu Fu sailed again. But he returned saying that a sea monster had blocked his path, and that he'd need 1,000 archers to defeat the beast. Again the emperor granted his request, and again Xu Fu headed off into the distance, but this time never to return.

WHAT HAPPENED NEXT?

Some people believe Xu Fu reached Japan and became an emperor. And the Emperor of China? He died when one of his men gave him a potion of eternal life...which was actually poisonous!

VOYAGES WEST

The Vikings traveled thousands of miles across the ocean in sturdy longships, crossing from Norway to Iceland, Greenland, and North America.

"I shall call this land Vinland, after its qualities."

—LEIF ERIKSSON

LEIF ERIKSSON

The year was 1000 AD, and Leif was following in his father's footsteps. Together with a small crew, he navigated across the Atlantic Ocean and landed in North America—in what is now known as Newfoundland in Canada. The Vikings named it Vinland, after its grape-producing meadows. Leif established at least one settlement on the new land but returned to Greenland after battles with Native Americans.

ERIK THE RED

Fifteen years before his son's voyage, Erik the Red (named for his red beard and fiery temper) was exiled from Norway and Iceland. He sailed west, discovering a land that he named The Green Land due to its excellent resources. This sweet-sounding name encouraged 500 men to follow with farm animals and building materials, and villages and towns were established.

"People will be attracted thither, if the land has a good name."

—ERIK THE RED

EASTERN EXPEDITIONS

While the Vikings are most famous for their epic voyages west, they actually sailed further to the east. They navigated the seas and rivers of Europe, raiding and trading along the way.

A NEW WORLD

European geographers knew that the Earth was round, so they thought that by sailing east to reach Asia, they'd also be able to sail west. When they tried to do this, they accidentally discovered America, which at first they assumed must be connected to Asia!

CHRISTOPHER COLUMBUS

In 1492, an Italian named Christopher Columbus convinced the Spanish court to sponsor him to sail westward, toward Japan. His ship, the *Santa Maria*, was one of the finest sailing ships of its age. When they reached land, an incredible cross-cultural conversation took place between Columbus and the local Taino people, with both sides exchanging gifts. Columbus thought he was in Asia and called the people Indians; he was actually in the Caribbean islands off the mainland of America. He made three further voyages but never knew he'd landed on a whole new continent!

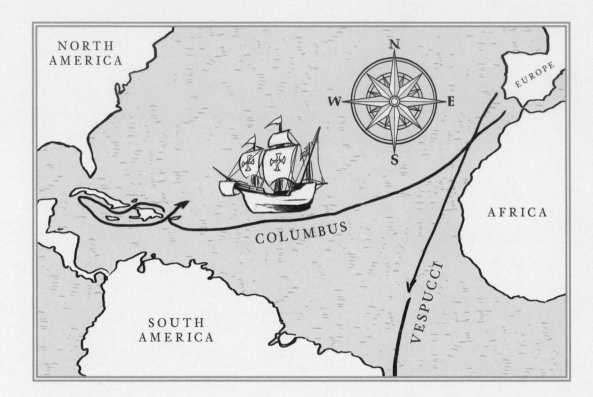

AMERIGO VESPUCCI

That honor lay with Amerigo Vespucci, another Italian navigator. Between 1497 and 1504, Vespucci made up to four return voyages across the Atlantic Ocean. He saw that the landmass was much bigger than anyone had realized and sailed down the coast of South America, sighting the mouth of the Amazon and Orinoco Rivers. He realized that the "New World" was not connected to Asia at all. A mapmaker labeled the continent America, after Vespucci's first name.

AROUND AFRICA

For more than two millennia, southern Africa remained a mystery to mapmakers. People had traveled overland to India, but was there a sea route that went around the tip of Africa? If so, someone could bring back spices and make a fortune in the process.

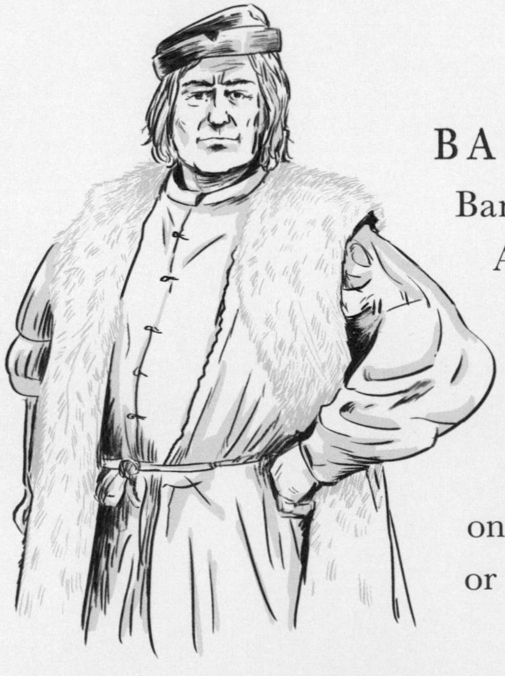

BARTOLOMEU DIAS

Bartolomeu Dias set sail around Africa in 1487, eventually sailing around the southern tip of Africa without realizing it at the time. However, his crew became fearful and demanded that he turn back. It was only then that he saw the "Cape of Storms," or the Cape of Good Hope as we now know it.

AFRICA

BARTOLOMEU DIAS

VASCO DE GAMA

INDIA

VASCO DE GAMA

A decade later, another Portuguese navigator, Vasco de Gama, sailed southward, seeking a sea route to India. His crew sailed around the Cape of Good Hope but couldn't pick up many supplies as the local chiefs were offended by the poor quality of their gifts. He sailed on to India, where the chiefs were equally unimpressed. He lost some ships in a monsoon on the return trip, but had sailed a greater distance than a complete circuit of the equator.

BEASTS AND PRIESTS

Myths abounded that Africa was full of strange beasts such as those pictured below. There was also the legend of Prester John—a Christian leader living on the other side of the land of the Muslims. Some mapmakers placed him in Asia and others in Africa—all were guessing! Neither Dias nor de Gama ventured far inland, and these myths continued for centuries.

Monopod (man with only one leg)

Panotti (man with giant ears)

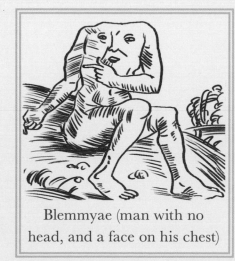

Blemmyae (man with no head, and a face on his chest)

Cynocephali (barking man with a dog's head)

AROUND THE WORLD

Who would be the first person to circle the globe? In the 1500s, this became a serious possibility. People had sailed around Africa, and had identified the tip of South America. Adventurers needed a combination of skill and luck to have any chance of success. Among many explorers from Europe, few people know that an Asian man was possibly the first person to sail around the world.

ENRIQUE

In 1511, a Portuguese explorer named Magellan was in the Malaysian region and capturing locals. Among those taken back to Europe was a man named Enrique, an excellent navigator. Eight years later, Magellan set sail on a grand expedition around the world with Enrique at the wheel. Eventually, they arrived at Cebu in the Philippines, just 125 miles (200 km) short of Enrique's home. Magellan quarreled with locals and was killed. Enrique didn't continue without his boss, but as he was so close to home, many think that Enrique found a ship and completed the first circumnavigation.

FRANCIS DRAKE

Francis Drake was the exact opposite of Enrique—a wealthy Englishman and a catcher and trader of slaves. He was also a great navigator and set off in 1577 to circle the world. At times, he acted as a pirate, raiding other ships and tormenting his enemies. He may not have been the kindest man, but he was skilled at finding the right winds and keeping his ship on course. In three years he returned to England, where he was treated as a hero and given a knighthood. History doesn't record such an honor for Enrique, though there is a statue in Malaysia commemorating his epic voyage.

"It isn't that life ashore is distasteful to me. But life at sea is better."

—*Francis Drake*

FRANCISCO DE ORELLANA

Chasing riches of cinnamon and gold, Spanish explorer Francisco de Orellana set off from Quito, Ecuador, in 1541. Instead of riches he found water—lots of it. Unable to continue on foot, his men built a boat and then another bigger one, which they sailed and paddled downstream in search of food. After six months, de Orellana had traveled the length of the Amazon and arrived at the Atlantic Ocean, where he was declared a hero.

AMAZONIAN

Great rivers deserve great stories, and the Amazon doesn't disappoint. Which brave explorers could navigate its many twists and turns and avoid piranhas, crocodiles, mosquitoes, and more?

ADVENTURES

LOPE DE AGUIRRE

Another Spaniard, Lope de Aguirre, followed in de Orellana's footsteps, searching for gold in the Amazon a few years later. He, too, failed in this mission, but succeeded in navigating the length of the river and declared himself the King of Peru. His crew declared him insane and ran as far away from him as possible!

PERCY FAWCETT

Englishman Percy Fawcett set off into the Amazon in 1925, hunting for gold. Instead of taking the famous explorer Lawrence of Arabia, he took his son Jack, a friend, and two local guides. The expedition was a disaster—they got eaten alive by insects, and Fawcett decided to send the guides home. They carried a letter to his wife stating "You have no fear of any failure," but neither father nor son were ever heard from again.

SOUTHERN SEAS

The southern seas are the furthest seas from Europe, and so it is no surprise that this region didn't receive any European visitors until relatively late. A Dutchman in the 1640s and an Englishman in the 1760s and 1780s were among the first, and they both brought back tales of wonderful lands and plants and animals unlike anything else on Earth.

AN ABLE SEAMAN

The Dutch sent explorer Abel Tasman out to the southern seas in search of great riches. He sailed around New Guinea and Australia, and his sighting of a southern island gave Tasmania its western name. He was the first European to see New Zealand, but his encounter with the local Maori didn't go peacefully—after the two sides traded shouts and then blasts on trumpet-like instruments, he opened fire and killed some locals, sparking centuries of distrust.

CAPTAIN COOK

Captain James Cook was one of history's greatest captains and navigators, adding more than 5,000 miles (8,000 km) of unknown coastline to maps in his first voyage alone. He sailed further south than anyone in written record, charted the waters of Australia, New Zealand, and the South Pacific, and gave accounts of numerous tribes. Unfortunately, he was a rather forceful man, and not all of these encounters were peaceful. He was the first European to land on Hawaii but was killed by locals.

"Ambition leads me as far as I think it is possible for me to go."

—CAPTAIN COOK

TROUBLE IN PARADISE

Few charts existed of the southern seas around Australia and New Guinea—these waters were known to be dangerous with sharks, rocks, reefs, strong currents, and unpredictable weather. Even the biggest ships traveled with caution. It is astonishing therefore that two crews steered safely through these waters in what were basically little rowboats.

MARY BRYANT

In the late 1700s in England, convicted criminals were sent to Australia. Mary Bryant was on a prison ship after being caught stealing and suffered greatly on the long voyage. When she arrived, she stole a boat and steered it through the open ocean on a 66-day voyage. She landed on Timor, where she claimed to be shipwrecked. However, the police realized who she was and sent her back to England, where she eventually found freedom.

WILLIAM BLIGH

Englishman William Bligh was captain of a ship called *Bounty*, which traveled to Tahiti for exotic fruits. Some crew members thought Bligh was too quick to punish them, and eventually, the crew mutinied and cast Bligh and his few supporters adrift in a tiny boat. Their chances of survival seemed slim, but Bligh managed to guide the boat more than 4,000 miles (6,500 km) from Tonga through the tropics to the safety of Timor.

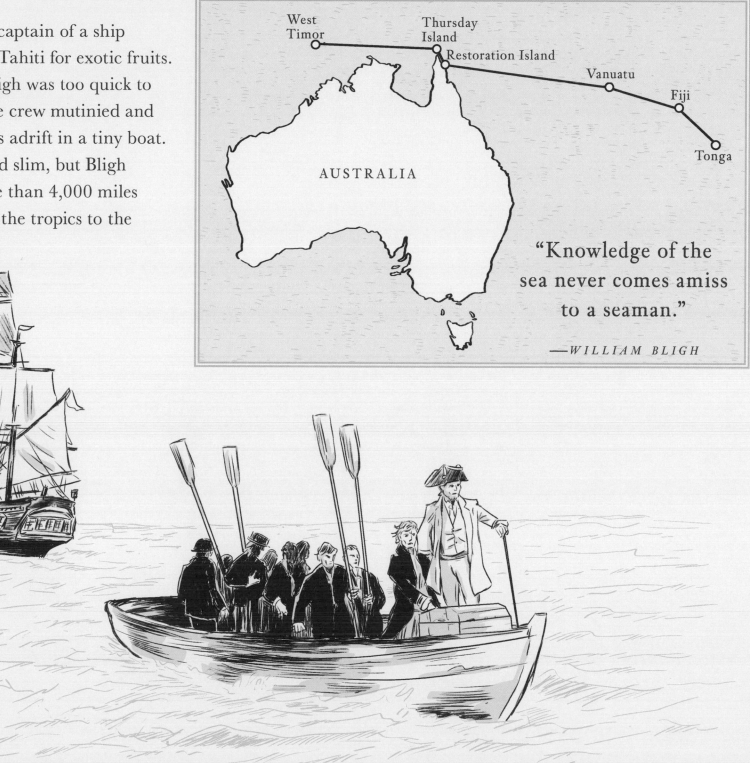

AUSTRALIA

West Timor · Thursday Island · Restoration Island · Vanuatu · Fiji · Tonga

"Knowledge of the sea never comes amiss to a seaman."

—*WILLIAM BLIGH*

THE NATURALISTS

Two great admirers of nature set off on two great journeys, drawing, cataloging, and marveling at the plants and animals they saw in tropical locations. When they arrived home, they changed the way we think about the world. The first of these naturalists was named Alexander von Humboldt, and the second was named Charles Darwin.

ALEXANDER VON HUMBOLDT

German Alexander von Humboldt was an expert in plant sciences. During travels in South America (1799–1804), he discovered new rivers, plants, animals, and tribes. He was shocked (literally!) by electric eels, but he always stuck to the facts when reporting new species. He was a talented artist, and his realistic sketches paved the way for future scientists. He was also a prolific author.

Anguloa orchid

Howler monkey

CHARLES DARWIN

During a five-year, around-the-world voyage on *The Beagle* (1831–1836), Darwin noticed similarities and differences in animals and birds of the Galapagos Islands. He started thinking that they were like branches of a tree… and that the different creatures had evolved from a common ancestor. This theory of evolution applied to humans, too—but this thinking was met with great hostility in Europe before becoming widely accepted and famous over time.

1. Large ground finch

2. Medium ground finch

3. Small ground finch

4. Green warbler finch

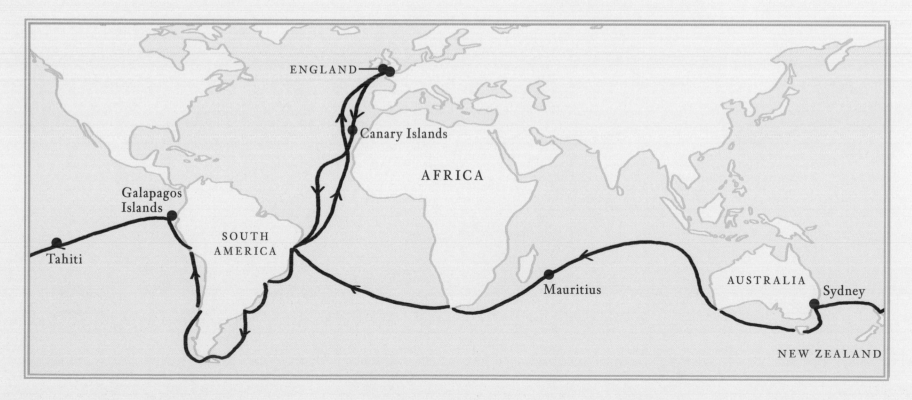

ENGLAND

Canary Islands

AFRICA

Galapagos Islands

SOUTH AMERICA

Tahiti

Mauritius

AUSTRALIA

Sydney

NEW ZEALAND

RUNNING RIVERS

Rivers act as roads for boats and allow travelers to head deep into wild places that are inaccessible by foot. But before rivers were mapped, travel along these uncharted waters could be dangerous and unpredictable—there were rapids, piranhas, crocodiles, and hostile tribes to negotiate.

A GRAND ADVENTURE—THE COLORADO

As adventurers go, John Wesley Powell certainly looked the part with his big bushy beard, explorer's hat, and one arm missing from a previous incident. And his location for exploration was a good choice, too—he was going to be the first white man to navigate the Grand Canyon and all its rapids. It was a perilous mission, and when he stumbled back into civilization, everyone said that they'd given up hope of finding him, and had written about his brave death in the newspapers!

INTO UNKNOWN ASIA— THE MEKONG AND YANGTZE

Frenchman Francis Garnier was part of a team who explored the mysterious Mekong River in Southeast Asia. The geography of the Mekong, which is the 12th-longest river in the world, was barely known to Europeans as the river passed through thick jungle country. Although not at first officially in charge, Garnier sketched most of the scenery, wrote most of the journals, and made most of the decisions. By the end of the trip, he was declared the leader and commanded his men to explore the Yangtze River in China—the longest river in Asia.

AN ENGLISHWOMAN IN AFRICA— THE OGOOUÉ

Mary Kingsley may have looked like a typical Victorian woman, but she led a colorful life in which she paddled up swamps, climbed mountains, and survived encounters with wildlife and cannibals in the wilds of West Africa. She explored the Ogooué River (in what is now Gabon) in a simple canoe, and hit a crocodile on the snout with her oar when it came too close before wrestling with a leopard and collecting samples of new species of fish and insects. Her book, *Travels in West Africa*, became a best seller.

KON-TIKI

Most people thought the Polynesians arrived from Asia, but a man named Thor Heyerdahl believed they could have sailed from South America. So, he built a raft using ancient materials and technology to test his theory.

> "If all's well, why worry?"
>
> —*Thor Heyerdahl*

SETTING OFF

Thor recruited five men and a Spanish-speaking parrot. He had no experience with sailing and couldn't even swim! However, he selected nine of the strongest balsawood trunks in Ecuador and lashed them together, then built a bamboo cabin with a roof made of banana leaves. They smashed a coconut against the boat instead of champagne, naming it *Kon-Tiki*, and set off in 1947.

THE OPEN OCEAN

Life on the open ocean was both difficult and magical. Using the stars to navigate, they spent nights gazing into the beauty of the skies. Overnight, several flying fish landed on the deck, which saved them from having to hunt! Sadly, the parrot was lost in a storm, but all of the men were fine. After 101 days at sea, they landed in Tahiti, proving that ancient technology was capable of making journeys between South America and Polynesia.

"I am prepared to go anywhere, provided it be forward."

—DAVID LIVINGSTONE

LAND

Overland journeys can be exhausting—there may be physical obstacles to cross, such as mountains, deserts, and swamps, or language and cultural barriers to cross when traveling far from home. Whether using camel, horse, foot, or other means, these hardy travelers rarely had signposts, yet somehow reached their destinations. Spanning 45 centuries, these trailblazers have much in common: a sense of adventure, a sense of direction, respect for Mother Nature, and a vast amount of determination.

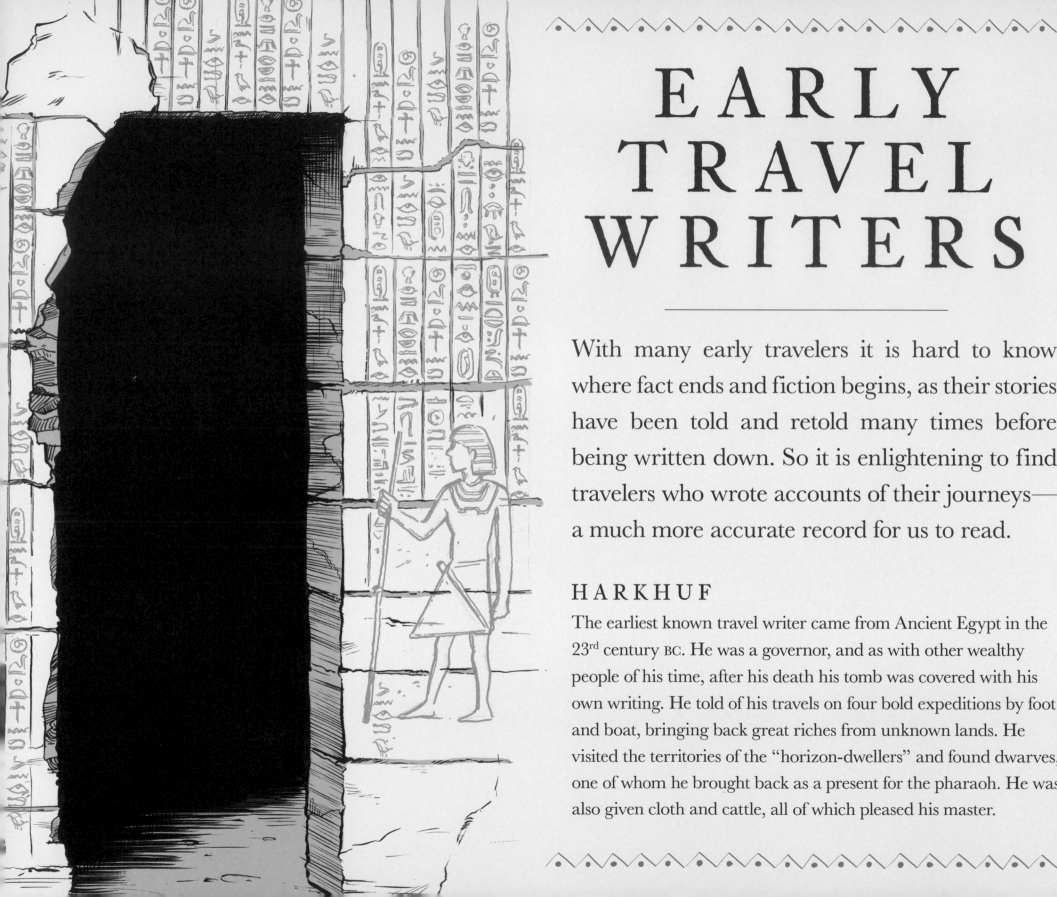

EARLY TRAVEL WRITERS

With many early travelers it is hard to know where fact ends and fiction begins, as their stories have been told and retold many times before being written down. So it is enlightening to find travelers who wrote accounts of their journeys— a much more accurate record for us to read.

HARKHUF

The earliest known travel writer came from Ancient Egypt in the 23rd century BC. He was a governor, and as with other wealthy people of his time, after his death his tomb was covered with his own writing. He told of his travels on four bold expeditions by foot and boat, bringing back great riches from unknown lands. He visited the territories of the "horizon-dwellers" and found dwarves, one of whom he brought back as a present for the pharaoh. He was also given cloth and cattle, all of which pleased his master.

PETRARCH

It would be another 1,500 years before "modern" travel writing—traveling purely for pleasure and not for trade, discovery, or war. An early record of such writing comes from an Italian named Petrarch, who climbed Mont Ventoux in France in 1336. He states that he climbed for the pleasure of seeing the mountaintop. Those who stayed at the bottom he called *frigida incuriositas* ("people with a cold lack of curiosity")!

ZHANG QIAN

Born in China in about 160 BC, Zhang Qian ("jang chee-an") was a great Chinese explorer and diplomat, as well as a writer. He set off westward in 139 BC with about 100 men, but they were captured by warriors from the Hun tribe. During 10 years of captivity, Zhang Qian learned the local language. When he finally escaped, he explored the western lands again, and brought back the first written records of the Ancient Silk Road—a trading corridor linking China and Central Asia.

ACROSS THE ALPS

Hannibal was a Carthaginian general with a plan—to attack the mighty Romans using war elephants. There was one problem: the Alps lay in the way—surely a team of 40 elephants couldn't cross this mountain range...could they?

TWO POWERFUL CITIES

Rome was growing in power. But the city of Carthage on the North African coast was powerful, too—it had captured some islands off the coast of Italy that Rome claimed. These two states could not agree, so they went to war. After 20 years of fighting, neither side really won, and things cooled down a little, but everyone expected a second war. Gladiators couldn't just shake hands—that wasn't how things worked.

ATTACK AND REVENGE

Hannibal became a great general for the Carthaginians. He captured many cities in Spain, using tricks such as tossing live snakes onto enemy ships to make them surrender. The Romans hated Hannibal so they decided to attack his home city of Carthage. As Hannibal was in Spain he was unable to defend Carthage, so he thought the best thing to do was to attack Rome. To do this, he needed to cross the icy Alps....

ELEPHANTS AND ALPS

In 218 BC Hannibal marched up to 40,000 men, 8,000 horses, and 40 war elephants toward the mountains in autumn. Few thought he could succeed. Half of his men and animals died in the bitter cold. But half succeeded, and a herd of elephants smashing into the enemy was a frightening prospect. Could Hannibal win the battle? Sadly not—their heroics had been used up in the journey, but what an incredible journey it was, reminding the Romans that almost anything was possible.

> "I shall either find a way or make one."
>
> —HANNIBAL

THE FAR, FAR EAST

Asia was a mysterious land for Europeans. Myths were common, and few knew what was going on at the other end of the great Eurasian landmass, except that fearsome Mongolian warriors had conquered half the world. Who would be brave enough to venture into these faraway lands?

MARCO POLO

Marco Polo was born into a family of merchants in Venice in 1254. His father and uncle were away from home, trading in Asia, and only met Marco when he was 15. They invited him on their next great trip two years later. Together, they traveled an astonishing 10,000 miles (15,000 km) over 24 years, bringing news from some of the least-known corners of Asia. Marco traveled from the Black Sea and Central Asian states to India, Sri Lanka, and China. Imprisoned back in Venice, Marco wrote about his fantastic journeys in his *Book of the Marvels of the World*, which became a best seller.

> "It seemed that I had been transported into another world."
>
> —*Friar William*

FRIAR WILLIAM

In 1248 Friar William from Flanders (Belgium) was sent by the Pope to the Mongolian capital of Karakorum to persuade the chiefs to become Christian. He rode for hundreds of miles on the back of a mule, staying with local people in their tents. He observed them carefully, and noted how they loved drinking milky alcohol, while he preferred cookies. When he arrived at Karakorum, he was astonished to see a city of great buildings as well as nomadic tents—and he found captured and free people from all around the world. He had a great religious debate with the Mongolian chief, but the Mongols had already conquered half of the known world, so they didn't need an extra god on their side!

IBN BATTUTA

In 1325, a young man set out from his home in Morocco to undertake the *hajj*, the journey to Mecca that all Muslims should make in their life. However, he kept going after Mecca, and during the next 24 years, visited many countries, becoming the world's greatest traveler.

THE *HAJJ*

Ibn Battuta came from a wealthy family, and when he set out on his *hajj*, he decided to visit new places and study along the way. He visited Tunis, Cairo, Alexandria, Jerusalem, and Damascus, never traveling along the same road twice. At Mecca, he saw pilgrims from many countries, and he decided to visit these exotic lands.

ONWARD

From Mecca he traveled across the desert to Baghdad. He then sailed to Mombasa before returning to the Middle East and on to the Black Sea. In Constantinople, the Byzantine Emperor gave him a horse, a saddle, and a parasol. He then traveled through Central Asia and Afghanistan, and on to India.

I'LL BE THE JUDGE OF THAT!

In India and the Maldives, Ibn Battuta was asked to be a judge because of his Islamic scholarship and his experience of the world. He spent eight years working in the courts, and met more than 40 heads of state during his travels. He went on to China—his first big step outside of the Muslim world—but met with disaster when his ship full of treasures for the emperor sank.

RETURN AND WRITINGS

In 1349, he finally returned home. But he was soon off again on further trips to Islamic Spain and the ancient desert city of Timbuktu, returning home again in 1354. This time, he wrote a book about his travels. The title was *Gift to Observers, Dealing with the Curiosities of Cities and the Wonder of Journeys*, but it is commonly known simply as *The Travels*. It is an astonishing book by an astonishing traveler.

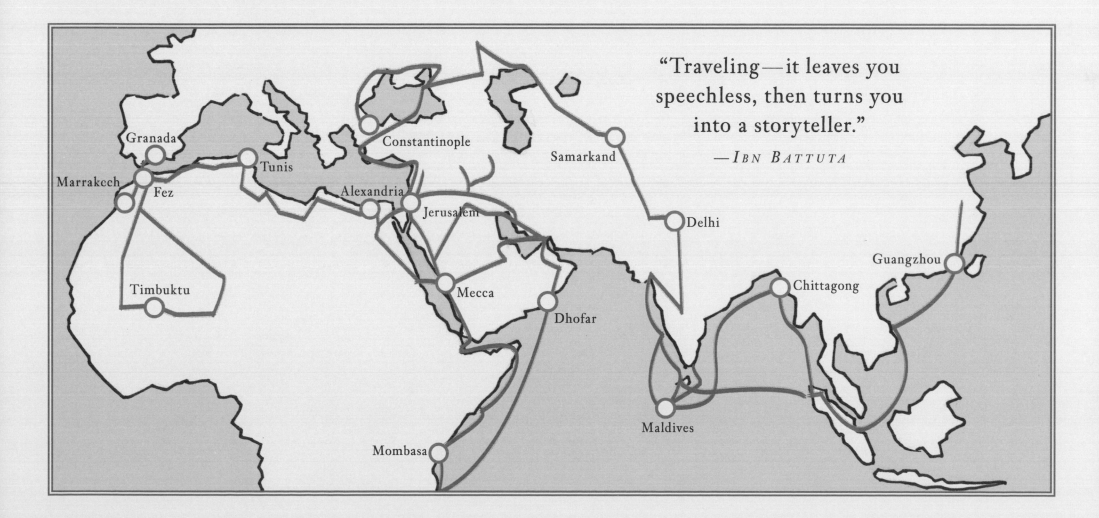

"Traveling—it leaves you speechless, then turns you into a storyteller."
—IBN BATTUTA

TO TIMBUKTU

In the heart of West Africa lies a beautiful city made of mud. To residents, it was once a wealthy center of trade, industry, and education. To outsiders, it seemed totally inaccessible, blocked by the Sahara. For much of its history, the city was closed to non-Muslims. In the 1700s and 1800s, Europeans craved to reach this mysterious city. Many died trying....

"I am the son of the road, my country is the caravan, my life the most unexpected of voyages."
—*LEO AFRICANUS*

LEO AFRICANUS

Joannes Leo Africanus (also known as al-Hasan ibn Muhammad al-Wazzan al-Fasi) was one of the earliest outsiders to reach the city. Born in Islamic Spain in 1494, he became a diplomat and geographer. He traveled across Africa, Europe, and the Middle East. In his book *A Description of Africa*, he notes that the inhabitants of Timbuktu are very rich: "instead of coined money, gold nuggets are used."

ALEXANDER GORDON LAING

In 1825, a determined Scotsman set out for Timbuktu. He had already figured out where the source of the Niger River was located, so he had a track record of African exploration. He set out across the Sahara Desert using camel caravans and local guides. All went well until he fought with locals and lost his right arm in the skirmish. Barely alive, he made it to Timbuktu, but sadly was murdered in the desert before he could report his findings.

RENÉ CAILLIÉ

Two years later, Frenchman René Caillié set out. He traveled disguised as an Egyptian making his way home. He did so on a camel caravan until he reached a town on the Niger River. From there he was able to pay a boatman to take him to Timbuktu. Unlike Laing, he lived to tell the tale, and received 10,000 francs and a gold medal when he returned to France.

THE WILD, WILD WEST

The American West was a great wilderness area, with mountains, forests, deserts, and great plains. Americans Lewis and Clark set out to fill in the gaps on the map. But the greatest traveler of their party was a Native American woman named Sacagawea.

1. LEWIS AND CLARK

President Thomas Jefferson invited Meriwether Lewis to take part in an expedition across the American West. Lewis was only 29, and had limited experience, so he approached his old army boss, William Clark, with a proposal: they would be jointly in charge of the expedition, and absolute equals.

3. A BUSY WILDERNESS!

As the mission progressed, Sacagawea guided them through the wilderness by communicating with people using Native American Hand Talk—a universal sign language. Lewis and Clark realized that the "wilderness" area was actually busy—they saw many Native American camps, and spotted 62 grizzly bears, none of which harmed them!

2. SACAGAWEA

The explorers soon ventured off into very remote areas. A Shoshone Indian tribeswoman, Sacagawea, joined the mission with her baby son, and she opened many doors for the explorers. Instead of fearing the white men, because Sacagawea and her baby were with them, everyone could see that they came in peace.

4. FROM SEA TO SHINING SEA

Eventually, the team found Sacagawea's Shoshone tribe, who provided horses and food for the party. But as they crossed the snowy Rocky Mountains, food ran out, and the team only survived by eating the horses. They continued by river and eventually reached the Pacific Ocean—they'd crossed an entire continent!

A SENSE OF THE WORLD

James Holman traveled more than 150,000 miles (400,000 km) in his lifetime—that's more than 10 times around the Earth! His distance record stood for more than a century—there's no doubt he was one of history's greatest travelers. And he was totally blind.

AN UNLIKELY RECORD BREAKER

Holman wasn't only blind—he also had severe rheumatism that caused leg pains. He sometimes couldn't get out of bed and often had to hobble around using a walking stick. His health problems began while in the Royal Navy, and he was transferred back to land as a Naval Knight—an injured sailor who would be taken care of at Windsor Castle. But Holman didn't like being taken care of one bit, so he told his doctor that he needed to go to France for fresh air and sunshine.

EUROPE

Rather than taking a luxurious cruise, Holman went to France on a standard ferry in 1819, then flagged down horses and carriages to take him across the countryside. He didn't speak a word of French! He loved the ride and all the sounds and smells. At times, he held on to a piece of rope tied to the carriage so he could run behind it for exercise! He felt refreshed and alive and decided to tour Italy, Switzerland, Germany, and the Netherlands, too.

RUSSIA

But Europe was not enough—Holman wanted to travel all around the world. Few thought Holman could make such a journey across some of the world's worst roads. Russians laughed at his plans when he arrived in Moscow and St. Petersburg, but he bought a small cart and found a driver, and rode through swamps and ice, sometimes hearing prison-gangs in chains, sometimes wild bears, and almost always hungry mosquitoes! In Siberia, he was arrested on suspicion of being a British spy. He was forced to turn around.

AROUND THE WORLD

Of course, Holman found another way. He sailed to places including Africa, South America, Sri Lanka, China, and Australia and never lost his sense of excitement about new places. He visited prisons, inspected mines, and opened new buildings. To prove himself to the crew of each new boat, he'd climb to the top of the mast—none of the sailors could imagine doing that while blind! He wrote best-selling books about his travels at the time, but sadly he is not well-known today, despite his incredible achievements.

IN SAHARAN SANDS

Great adventurers need great places to explore, and where could be a greater challenge than the Sahara Desert? The climate was harsh and the locals were generally quite hostile. But Heinrich Barth was no ordinary explorer.

1. A STUDENT OF PEOPLE

Born in Germany in 1821, Heinrich Barth was fascinated by people from different cultures from a young age, unlike many other explorers of Africa, who were more interested in maps, glory, gold, colonies, or even slavery. He studied many languages before setting off for Africa. Officially his task was to catalog the people and places in the vast regions of the Central Sahara and Sudan. For Barth, this was a dream job.

2. A SOLO TRAVELER

Barth was part of a team of three, but when his companions fell ill and died, Barth continued alone, and for five years, he traveled more than 10,000 miles (16,000 km) through remote parts of Africa. He explored ancient camel-trading routes, oasis towns, desert, cattle-herding country, and the tented life of the Tuareg nomads. He grew thick whiskers on his face, and he must have been an astonishing sight for the North Africans!

3. AN EQUAL AND A FRIEND

He was always prepared to stop and talk with locals so that he could understand more about the lands he passed through. In Timbuktu he was received by the king, and they talked about faraway places. Friendships were formed wherever he went, and he treated everyone as an equal—a far cry from other European travelers at that time. He spoke five African languages fluently and could get by in another dozen or so.

4. DR. BARTH, I PRESUME?

Because he visited remote places for months at a time, it was difficult to send news back to Europe. After a long time without any word, it was assumed that he had died, and a search party was organized. Barth was absolutely astonished when he met a European who had been sent to look for his coffin! We can only imagine he was met with the words "Dr. Barth, I presume?" at the end of his incredible adventures!

THE PONY EXPRESS

The wild, wild West was a vast expanse of wilderness. Blizzards, dust storms, and head-hunters were some of the many perils, but the bravest adventurers in America were attracted by advertisements like this:

"WANTED: Expert riders, willing to risk death daily...."

CROSSING A CONTINENT

The Pony Express was a network of horses, men, and staging posts that transferred mail halfway across America, from Missouri to California. The 2,000-mile (3,000-km) course crossed the Great Plains, the Rocky Mountains, and the Sierra Nevada Mountains and took 10 days to complete.

JOHNNY FRY

Beginning in April 1860, Johnny Fry was one of the first riders. He was young and athletic, with a sense of adventure. He sped across the plains before handing to the next rider. A team of about 100 men rode in all weather conditions and were taught to value the mail pouch more than their lives!

SPECIAL DELIVERY

Henry Brown was born in 1816 in Virginia. His parents were slaves and so was he, though he always dreamed of freedom. Little did he know that one day his dream would come true in spectacular fashion.

A LIFE OF SERVICE

Henry Brown worked on a tobacco farm. It was backbreaking work under the hot Sun, with the threat of a whip if he didn't work hard enough. But Henry was an optimistic man and made the best of what he had. Still, he hated his position as a slave and wanted a change. When a new owner bought his wife and children and took them away from him, he knew he had to try to escape, even if he died in the process....

THE GREAT ESCAPE

A friend had contacts in Philadelphia, a city that opposed slavery. They formed a plan—Henry could be mailed in a wooden box to his freedom! Henry cut one of his fingers badly, then showed his injury to his owner to get a few days off from work. A box was made—smaller than a coffin—and Henry was mailed off! He spent 27 hours trapped inside, some of the time standing on his head when people ignored the sign that read "THIS WAY UP." Eventually he reached Philadelphia and sang a song of thankfulness as he stepped out of the box and tasted freedom for the first time in his life.

CROSSING A

Australia is so big that most people consider it to be an entire continent rather than an island. It's a tremendous journey to walk across it from south to north or from west to east, but two very different groups of people achieved this astonishing journey in very different ways.

BURKE AND WILLS

In 1860 a party of 19 men, 27 camels, and 23 horses set off from Melbourne on a coast-to-coast walk through unknown territory. In the outback, leaders Robert Burke and William Wills decided that a team of four should attempt a sprint to the coast. The four passed through deserts before eventually spotting saltwater—the edge of Australia! Their return journey was a march from hell, and on their arrival the camp was empty except for a sign on a tree saying "DIG." Burke duly dug and found supplies and a note that the others had stayed for an extra month, but left the day before Burke's team had arrived! The men were so tired and ill from their journey that tragically three of them died—including Burke and Wills—before they could return to Melbourne.

CONTINENT

SONGLINES

People had been walking across Australia long before the time of Burke and Wills. The Aboriginal people of Australia had an amazing system to map their land using songs. When walking through the vast outback, people would sing a song about that journey, which included key geographical locations as well as legends and myths. Perhaps for 40,000 years, these songs have been passed down from one generation to the next.

IN HARMONY

The Aboriginal people live in harmony with nature, and are masters at reading the stories that nature has to tell, from animal tracks to weather patterns, and from signs of water nearby to methods of calming crocodiles. They must have been very puzzled by Burke and Wills making a mad dash through the country without reading the signs of Mother Nature!

PAINTING PLANTS

In Victorian times, it was assumed that women would become wives and then mothers. Marianne North had different ideas—she called marriage a "terrible experiment" and instead traveled through the world's wildest regions painting rare and exotic plants.

1. A DIFFERENT PATH

Marianne was the daughter of a British Member of Parliament and was expected to behave in certain ways. She did as she was told, but didn't want to marry and become a "servant" to a husband. To avoid pressure to marry from her father, she became his best friend and shared his enthusiasm for plants and travel. She traveled with him to Syria and the Nile from 1865 to 1867, and this taste of adventure gave her an appetite for more.

2. A PAINTER OF PLANTS

As a child, Marianne was more of a singer than an artist, but she took an oil-painting lesson and loved it. She then had all the elements she needed for her remarkable journeys—a love of plants, painting, and traveling. After her father's death in 1869, she was free from responsibilities and decided to travel the world, painting "the peculiar plants" that lived in some of the wildest places, far, far away from her home in England.

3. A WORLD OF FLOWERS

First on her world tour was America and then Jamaica, where she began a decade-long schedule of around-the-clock painting. North traveled to Brazil, Tenerife, Japan, Singapore, Borneo, Sri Lanka, India, and South Africa. At Darwin's suggestion, she took in Australia, New Zealand, and Tasmania, too. Whereas naturalists were digging up plants and shooting animals to bring back to London, North recorded each species perfectly in paint.

4. KEW GARDENS

When she returned, she asked the director of Kew Gardens whether she could build a gallery there to display her work and sell tea, coffee, and cookies. The director agreed to her gallery but refused permission to sell refreshments as it was a serious place of scientific study. Mischievously, North hung her paintings of tea and coffee plants above the entrance so that visitors were in fact offered tea and coffee in the gallery!

LIVINGSTONE
AND STANLEY

In 1871, two of Africa's greatest explorers met at Ujiji on the shore of Lake Tanganyika. It was there that one of history's most famous greetings—"Dr. Livingstone, I presume?"—*may* have been said. Who were these two explorers, and why did they meet in the heart of Africa?

1. DAVID LIVINGSTONE

David Livingstone was an explorer and a "medical missionary"—he'd provide medical support to people using Western methods and tell them about Christianity, too. He came from a poor family in Scotland, unlike many of the very wealthy explorers at the time. He wanted to end slavery but feared people wouldn't listen to his opinion unless he became the most famous African explorer of all. So he decided to search for the source of the River Nile, deep in the heart of the continent.

2. LOST, WE PRESUME

Livingstone first explored the Zambezi River before the Nile. He thought both would open up trade routes into the interior of Africa, and that trading of goods would replace the trading of people. He started his search for the source of the Nile from the island of Zanzibar, where he recruited local adventurers. He reached Lake Malawi, but most of his crew had returned home, and many of his medicines had been stolen. The crewmen who returned told people that Livingstone had died.

3. STANLEY AND THE MEETING

Henry Morton Stanley was a Welsh-born American who had been a soldier and then a sailor before becoming a journalist. His editor sent him to Africa to search for the legendary explorer Livingstone, who could still be alive. Stanley began his journey at Zanzibar, where he hired 111 men. They marched more than 600 miles (1,000 km) through tropical forests with deadly insects, before finally finding Livingstone alive at Ujiji, where the famous greeting was *possibly* given.

4. STANLEY SOLDIERS ON

Stanley then became an explorer in his own right. He mapped Lake Victoria and confirmed it to be one of the sources of the Nile, and he also explored the Congo River from source to sea. His blood must have tasted sour to mosquitoes, for while his colleagues—African and European—had a habit of dying from malaria, he stayed healthy. His crisscrossing of Central Africa and his breathtaking books made him a celebrity, and he is remembered as one of the greatest explorers of Africa.

PILGRIMAGE OF PEACE

Satish Kumar's entire life has been a remarkable journey. At age nine, he left home and became a monk in the Jain religion in India, but at 18 he ran away to find a new path. After working on farms and in politics, he decided to set out on his greatest journey yet.

FIRST STEPS

The year was 1962, and the world was experiencing a Cold War with a handful of countries building more and more nuclear weapons. The situation was potentially explosive, and Satish felt he couldn't just sit and watch without trying to do something. Together with a friend, he decided to set out on a peace walk, traveling to the leaders of the four main nuclear nations by foot and delivering his message that peace was a better path than war. The two men decided to travel without money and without eating meat—they would rely on the kindness of strangers and the power of vegetables throughout their journey.

A NICE CUP OF TEA

They received a warm welcome throughout Asia before heading toward Moscow. In Armenia they visited a tea factory, where a worker gave Satish four teabags to be handed to the leaders of the U.S., U.S.S.R., U.K., and France in the hope that if they ever felt like pressing the nuclear button, they would stop first and make a cup of tea. Maybe they'd change their minds.

"Difficulties are just things to overcome, after all."

—*Ernest Shackleton*

ICE *and* SNOW

The North and South Poles have acted as magnets to many great explorers. Their attraction is their remoteness and harsh conditions—only the strongest and bravest can hope to take journeys to the ends of the Earth and come back alive. While the physical poles have been the main attraction, others sought passages through icy waters—new routes that would link continents. And some dreamed of Everest, Tibet, and Greenland—mysterious places wrapped up in icy fortresses.

THE CABLE GUYS

In the 1860s, people dreamed of connecting the world with cables through which messages could be carried. News could travel in minutes rather than months, which would change the way the world worked. This huge project involved epic journeys on foot, dogsled, and horseback across some of the most remote regions of the world.

1. OPPORTUNITY

Following a failed attempt to lay a cable under the Atlantic Ocean, many people thought that an overland route would be better. This would go north through Alaska, under the Bering Strait, and down through the Russian Far East, linking with Vladivostok and with Chinese cables. The route traveled through unknown, roadless, frosty regions—brave men would be needed to map out the way.

2. UP THROUGH ALASKA

The Russian-American Telegraph Company was formed, and Perry Collins was its chief. Work began but conditions were tough. Fires had to be lit to melt the ice before each telegraph pole could be sunk into the ground. But work continued, and the cable was soon put to use to carry news of President Abraham Lincoln's assassination to the workers.

3. THROUGH UNKNOWN LANDS

On the Russian side, one of the workers was 20-year-old George Kennan. He had no experience and did not speak the local languages. However, he had a big sense of adventure and a warm personality, which meant people trusted him. He traveled thousands of miles through the wilderness on sled, horseback, and foot, sometimes staying in the tents of nomads and other times camping out in the elements.

4. FAILURE...AND SUCCESS

In 1867, a successful cable was placed under the Atlantic. Messages could be sent between continents in minutes; a communication revolution had begun. The overland cable was not now needed, but ironically, the workers didn't hear the news for almost a year! Their work was not wasted, however, as they brought back knowledge of new lands and peoples.

THE NORTHWEST PASSAGE

FRANKLIN'S FAILURE

In 1845, Englishman John Franklin assembled fine boats and crew. He estimated that there was less than 300 miles (500 km) of unexplored coast. However, his boats got trapped in ice, and his men had to try to walk to safety. Sadly, there were no survivors from this voyage.

Europeans dreamed of a shortcut to Asia that would increase their access to silk and spices. Explorers sought a route across the top of the American continent —a mission that was to take 400 years.

AMUNDSEN ARRIVES

In 1903, Norwegian explorer Roald Amundsen decided to take a different approach—where earlier crews had taken big ships, many men, and tons of supplies, Amundsen would take a little boat, only six men, and as few supplies as he dared. He would stay close to the coastline and catch fish and seals to survive, learning from the experience of the local Inuit people. Although his boat got iced in, too, he was able to calmly wait until it melted, living with the locals and learning their skills. By 1906, he'd completed his voyage— he'd sailed the northwest passage.

THE NORTHEAST PASSAGE

After finding the northwest passage, explorers' thoughts turned to the northeast passage—could anyone sail across the top of Russia in the short summer months when the waters were ice-free? This, too, could be an important route for trade....

MODERN SUCCESS

Explorers Fridtjof Nansen and Vitus Bering were among the earliest to seek a northeast passage, and proved that a navigation would be possible. However, the honor of the first complete passage fell to Finnish-Swedish explorer Adolf Erik Nordenskiöld, who navigated from west to east in 1878 in the *Vega* expedition.

AN ANCIENT CROSSING

Portuguese captain David Melgueiro may have sailed across the northeast passage in the 1660s. His ship, *Pai Eterno* (Perpetual Father), is said to have traveled from Japan to Portugal via the Arctic Ocean. Weather data shows this was feasible—the summers of the years around 1660 were the warmest in two centuries, so an ice-free route could have been open.

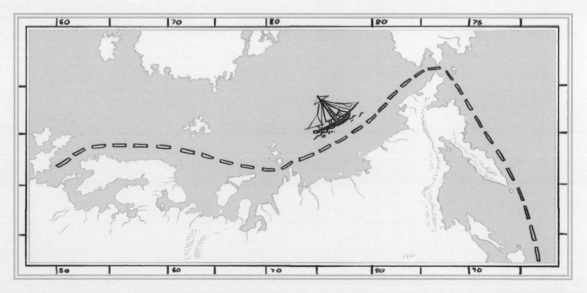

ROALD AMUNDSEN

Roald Amundsen had already successfully navigated the northwest passage. He picked a team of strong, fit men and carefully planned his expedition. He marked the first 150 miles (250 km) of his route with Norwegian ski flags and used dogs to haul his sleds. He wore furs that had been tested in extreme conditions. He'd trained in leading dog teams with Canadian Inuits. Although he loved the dogs dearly, he realized that to reach his goal, he would have to feed the weaker dogs to the stronger ones. Amundsen arrived at the South Pole on December 14, 1911, and raised the Norwegian flag.

RACE TO THE SOUTH POLE

To be the first to stand on the base of the world...that was the ultimate explorer's goal, and Antarctica became a magnet for explorers in the early 1900s. After others had failed, two teams set off in 1911 in what would become a tale of triumph and tragedy.

CAPTAIN SCOTT

Captain Robert Falcon Scott led a rival English expedition. Although he took a team of dogs, he had little experience in handling them and thought that ponies would be better for the job. He brought motorized sleighs but without the engineer who knew how to operate and fix them. The men's food lacked nutrition, and they marked their route less carefully than Amundsen, which was to prove deadly. Scott also made his men carry heavy rock samples. Despite all this, five brave men from Scott's party set off for the polar dash. They must have been heartbroken to see the Norwegian flag and a note from Amundsen. Tragically, the men got lost in blizzard conditions and perished on the ice just 11 miles (17 km) from safety.

I HAVE A DREAM

From a young age, Nobu Shirase dreamed of exploring Antarctica. He studied the polar regions while at temple school, and followed five rules throughout his life to prepare himself for extreme conditions: no alcohol, no tobacco, no tea, no drinking hot water, and no warming himself by the fire even in the cold. As an adult, it was difficult for Shirase to gain funding and recruit a crew, but he was very determined, and his dream became a reality.

SOUTHBOUND

In 1911, the *Kainin-Maru* set sail. It was half the size of the boats used by Scott and Amundsen, and when it docked in New Zealand for supplies, people questioned whether it could complete the journey. On the first attempt, the ship became blocked by sea ice, and Shirase had to turn around and winter in Australia until conditions improved. On the second attempt, the little ship landed on the Antarctic coast at the Bay of Whales, and the men set foot on the icy continent—the first Asians to do so.

FORGET ME NOT!

The dash to the South Pole is generally thought of as a two-horse race—the triumph of Roald Amundsen versus the tragedy of Captain Robert Falcon Scott. However, there was a third expedition on the frozen continent at the same time, led by Nobu Shirase ("noh-boo shih-rah-say") from Japan.

THE DASH PATROL

As one party surveyed the coastal area, a "dash patrol" headed southward inland. Using dog sleds driven by Ainu tribesmen, they made it to 80 degrees south and raised the Japanese flag. Despite harsh conditions, rock samples were collected, film was shot, coastal territory was mapped, and not a single life was lost.

FORGET ME NOT!

However, both Amundsen and Scott reached the South Pole (Amundsen's team ran into Shirase's coastal party on their way back), so many people have forgotten this third crew of brave men. Also, with growing concern around the world about Japanese military activity in Asia, the international newspapers were not kind to the Japanese expedition. In fact, it took 99 years before Shirase's expedition notes were published in English.

SHACKLETON'S JOURNEY

In one of the greatest adventure stories of all time, Shackleton's ship became trapped in polar ice, so he led his crew on a daring escape that took him over rough seas, and on a seemingly impossible overland journey so dangerous that no one had attempted it before and few have followed since.

"Through endurance we conquer."
—*Ernest Shackleton*

ANTARCTIC ADVENTURES

Irishman Ernest Shackleton was delighted to be chosen for Captain Scott's *Discovery* mission to the South Pole in 1901. Together with one other man, they made it as close to the South Pole as anyone had ever been at the time. Seven years later, Shackleton led his own expedition, where he succeeded in climbing Antarctica's highest mountain and getting even closer to the South Pole before having to turn back.

TRAPPED!

When Amundsen reached the South Pole in 1911, Shackleton set himself a new goal: to walk across the entire continent to create a new "first." In 1914, he set sail for Antarctica with his crew in a ship called *Endurance*. However, his ship became trapped in the ice. The crew waited patiently, but the pressure of the ice started cracking their boat, so they camped on the ice and removed the lifeboats before the ship finally sank.

ELEPHANT ISLAND

Shackleton and his men drifted on the ice with the lifeboats and supplies before launching into the wild seas. They were a long way from anywhere, so it was a miracle when every one of their boats reached dry land. But they were far from safety: they'd landed on uninhabited Elephant Island, more than 600 miles (1,000 km) away from the nearest human. They turned their lifeboats upside down to make huts and hunted seals and penguins to survive.

THE GREAT ESCAPE

Shackleton and five of his men set sail in a lifeboat for South Georgia, where they crossed more than 50 miles (80 km) of icy mountains to seek help. Shackleton took two men, and after 36 hours, they stumbled into a Norwegian whaling station, where they were welcomed as heroes. The men on South Georgia and Elephant Island were all rescued—not a single life was lost.

TO TIBET

Tibet lies high in the Himalaya Mountains. It is extremely difficult to reach, and foreign travelers were traditionally banned from visiting...which made them even more determined to do so! Most were turned back, but a few brave souls caught glimpses of this forbidden kingdom.

NAIN SINGH RAWAT

Nain Singh Rawat was born in a village in India famous for explorers and adventurers. He learned the Tibetan language and ventured into Tibet in 1865 disguised as a monk in order to make the first map of the region. He hid his map inside prayer wheels, and he used fake Tibetan "prayer beads" to count his steps so that he could measure the distances.

NIKOLAY PRZEWALSKI

Russian Nikolay Przewalski was an amazing explorer who traveled all across Central Asia. He gave his name to the world's only species of wild horse (which still roams free in Mongolia), and explored much of northern Tibet in 1872, but he was forced to turn back without reaching the magical city of Lhasa.

ANNIE TAYLOR

Annie Taylor became a missionary and wanted to travel to Lhasa to convert Tibetans to Christianity. She spent time learning the language and customs, then shaved off her hair and wore Tibetan clothing as a disguise. After four months of journey on horseback in the winter of 1893, Taylor saw Lhasa in the distance, but the Tibetans forced her to turn around, just short of her goal.

HEINRICH HARRER

Heinrich Harrer was an Austrian mountaineer on a climbing expedition with a friend in the Himalayas. When World War II broke out, the British Indians captured them, but they escaped and walked to Tibet. Harrer spent seven years in Tibet, met the Dalai Lama, and wrote a book about his adventures on the "Roof of the World."

ON TOP *of the* WORLD

Everest. The highest peak on Earth. It was finally conquered in 1953 by New Zealander Edmund Hillary and a Nepalese Sherpa named Tenzing Norgay. The journey from their everyday lives to the bottom of the mountain is at least as interesting as their record-breaking scramble to the top....

YAK HERDER

Tenzing Norgay was born in the foothills of Everest and took care of yaks for a living, with the mountain always in sight. His family lived among the Sherpa people in Nepal— a people who became famous for their extraordinary strength when climbing mountains. Because of this, Norgay was recruited by a Swiss expedition led by Raymond Lambert. Lambert noticed Norgay's incredible abilities and treated him as an equal. Together, they climbed to 28,215 feet (8,600 m)—higher than anyone had been before.

BEEKEEPER

Thousands of miles away, beekeeper Edmund Hillary loved climbing the Southern Alps in New Zealand. He read about George Mallory's brave attempts to climb Everest in the 1920s—he almost made it but vanished into thin air, assumed dead near the summit. News reached him that Lambert and Norgay had almost reached the top, too. So it was possible—it just needed the right men in the right place at the right time.

THE DREAM TEAM

Norgay and Hillary teamed up in 1953. Norgay possessed local knowledge and experience of the high reaches of Everest, and Hillary brought mathematical precision, always calculating the rate of climb and the amount of oxygen remaining. Also, they used the experience from the previous Swiss expeditions and knew exactly where to place their bases and supplies. Their final element of success was equipment—they were supplied with the latest high-tech gear, without which they wouldn't have reached the highest slopes.

ON TOP OF THE WORLD

The men spent the final night of the climb at 27,560 feet (8,400 m). The temperature was -17°F (-27°C), and they hardly slept. After a hot drink at 4 a.m., they set off, barely speaking to save precious oxygen. At 11 a.m., they stood on top of the world. Hillary held out his hand for Norgay to shake, but Norgay hugged him instead. Together they had achieved the impossible.

"It has been a long road."

—*TENZING NORGAY*

AN AFRICAN IN GREENLAND

Growing up in a mud-hut in Togo, a life of coconut-collecting and lizard-hunting awaited young Tété-Michel Kpomassie. When he chanced upon a book telling tales of a land of ice and snow, he made up his mind to travel to this faraway land.

AFRICA

One day, whilst high in a coconut palm, the teenage Tété-Michel was surprised by a snake and fell from the tree. He became ill and was taken to a priestess of the Snake Cult to rid him of this demon. Upon his recovery, Tété-Michel was to join the Snake Cult but while he was on the mend, he read a beautifully illustrated book about Greenland. He decided to find a way to get to this amazing place and he ran away from home soon after.

GREENLAND

Twelve years later, in the mid-1960s, Tété-Michel finally sailed to the land of his dreams and spent time with several Greenlandic families. Here he witnessed children being indulged by their parents—a far cry from the strict discipline of his own home. But as he traveled around the country, he saw more similarities than differences—friendly people with warm hearts and a love of good stories.

"Never interrupt someone doing something you said couldn't be done."
—AMELIA EARHART

MAN *and* MACHINE

Machines have helped mankind in all walks of life, and journeys are no exception. Since the invention of the wheel, humans have been dreaming up devices to help them travel further and faster...and occasionally with greater comfort. Great machines have been built to tackle land, sea, sky, and space, and a new breed of drivers, pilots, and mechanics have been born. Let's examine these high-tech explorers and their traveling contraptions.

AROUND
the
WORLD
on a
PENNY
FARTHING

The year was 1884. No one had ridden a bicycle across America, let alone around the world. Roads were scarce, and bandits were plentiful. Few thought Thomas Stevens had a chance of success when he set off with only a rain cape, a change of clothes, and a pocket revolver. Ahead lay vast roadless regions, baking deserts, hostile locals, and threatening wildlife.

AMERICA

Stevens first encountered the Sierra Nevada Mountains, then the Great Plains, with only wagon trails to follow. In places, he hopped onto the railroad track and rode over the bumpy wooden sleepers rather than bike across the rocky ground around him. For about a third of America, he walked, but he eventually made it to Boston.

EUROPE

In Europe, armies of local "wheelmen" escorted him through England, France, Germany, Austria, Hungary, Slavonia, Serbia, Bulgaria, Rumelia, and Turkey. The European roads were better, and he was in high spirits. He forged a friendship with a Hungarian cyclist, despite sharing no common language.

ASIA

Thomas rode through Turkey—racing villagers on horseback—and into Iran. The police in Afghanistan refused him entry, so he went back to Constantinople (now Istanbul) by boat, and then on to India. There, he continued on his bike through India and into China, where he was almost beaten to death. Finally, he crossed Japan.

THE END

Stevens returned home in 1886 to find that a small-wheeled "safety bicycle" had been developed, and two years later John Dunlop invented the air-filled tire. This meant the high-wheeler's days were numbered, so although he didn't know it at the time, Stevens gave the grandest bicycle the grandest of good-byes.

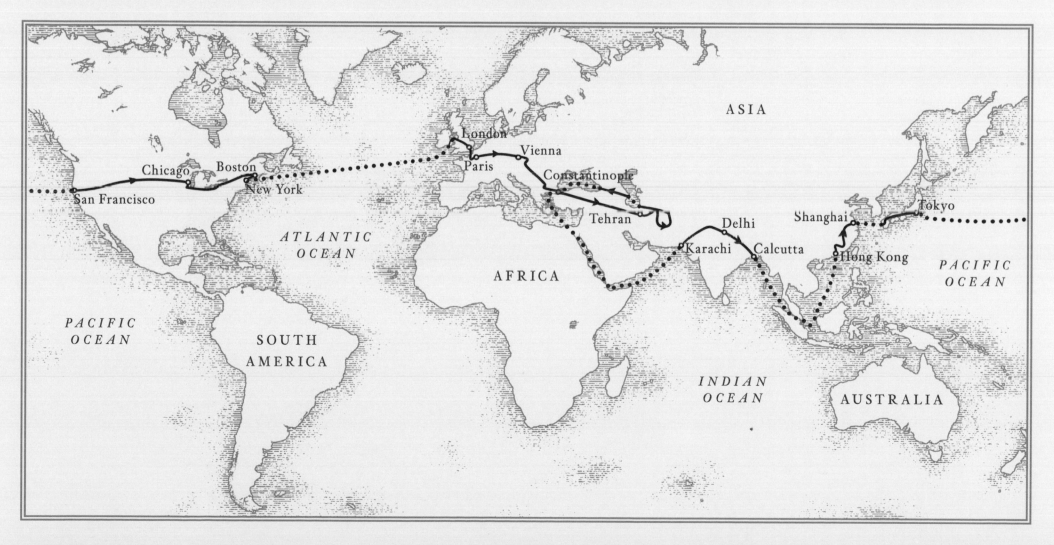

AROUND THE WORLD IN 72 DAYS

A SENSE OF ADVENTURE

Nellie Bly (real name Elizabeth Jane Cochran) was always an adventurous person. In her day, female journalists were rare, but she won a place at a newspaper in Pittsburgh. Her editor wanted her to focus on fashion and gardening, but instead she went to Mexico to gather sensational stories! Later, while working for another newspaper, she pretended to be insane so that she could write from inside a mental hospital. Very brave!

Jules Verne's book *Around the World in 80 Days* caused a sensation when it was published. The world had suddenly become a smaller place, thanks to new railways across America and India and the completion of the Suez Canal, which opened up a shorter sea route from Europe to Asia. It was only a matter of time before someone attempted a spectacular around-the-world trip.

THE RIGHT WOMAN FOR THE JOB

Nellie had a story idea: to try to beat the fictional 80-day around-the-world trip of Phileas Fogg in Jules Verne's book. Her editor liked the idea but felt it was a job for a man. "Very well," replied Nellie. "Start the man and I'll start the same day for some other newspaper and beat him." The newspaper could see Nellie's determination and decided to send her after all!

HALFWAY THERE

Nellie set off with few clothes and some gold and cash in a small bag tied around her neck. She sailed from New York to England, then to France, where she had tea with Jules Verne! On she went to Italy by train, then by ship to Egypt, Yemen, and on to Sri Lanka: she was halfway around the world, on course to smash the challenge.

A TRIUMPHANT RETURN

She sailed on to Malaysia, Singapore, and Hong Kong, then through stormy seas to Japan, and on from Yokohama to San Francisco. Crossing America by train, she received a hero's welcome at every city. When she arrived back in New York, she'd completed the journey in just 72 days.

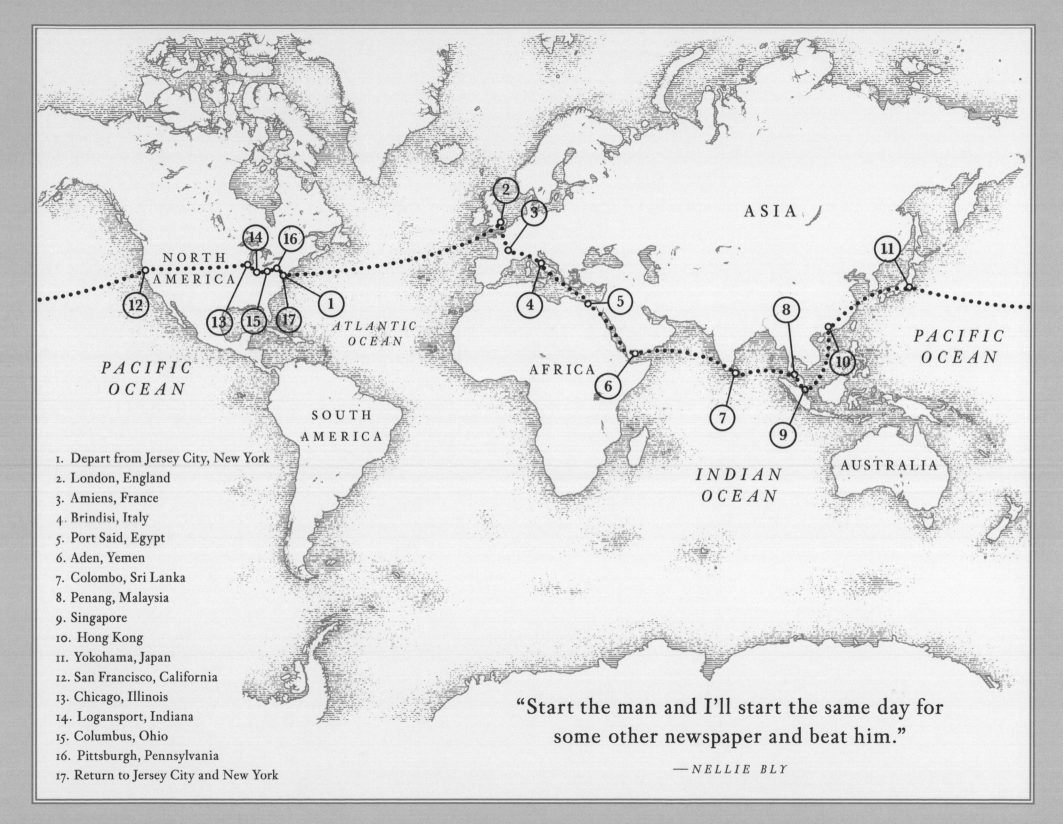

1. Depart from Jersey City, New York
2. London, England
3. Amiens, France
4. Brindisi, Italy
5. Port Said, Egypt
6. Aden, Yemen
7. Colombo, Sri Lanka
8. Penang, Malaysia
9. Singapore
10. Hong Kong
11. Yokohama, Japan
12. San Francisco, California
13. Chicago, Illinois
14. Logansport, Indiana
15. Columbus, Ohio
16. Pittsburgh, Pennsylvania
17. Return to Jersey City and New York

"Start the man and I'll start the same day for some other newspaper and beat him."
—NELLIE BLY

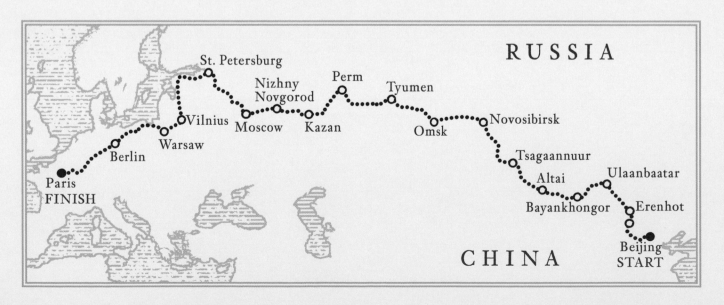

THE GREAT RACE

In 1907, the motor car was still a novelty. Vehicles were loud and clunky and only owned by the very wealthy. They usually broke down after a short distance. Some people wanted to know if the car was destined to be a useful invention or just a toy for the rich. There was one way to find out....

PEKING TO PARIS

When a French newspaper announced a race from Peking (now Beijing) to Paris, only five teams lined up for the start in China— three from France, one from the Netherlands, and one from Italy, the last of which was driven by a prince, a journalist, and a mechanic.

ACROSS THE GOBI DESERT

In China, cars were a total novelty! Fuel was sent ahead on camels, and the cars had to be pushed on mountain roads. In Mongolia, the cars became thirsty for fuel and water, and in the Gobi Desert, one of the teams gave up the race.

SIBERIAN SWAMPS

In Siberia they encountered swamps and bogs, and roads were mostly non-existent. At times the drivers' only option was to drive along the track of the Trans-Siberian Railway, bumping over the wooden sleepers. The Italian team suffered a bridge breaking while they crossed it and had to rescue their car from an upside-down position!

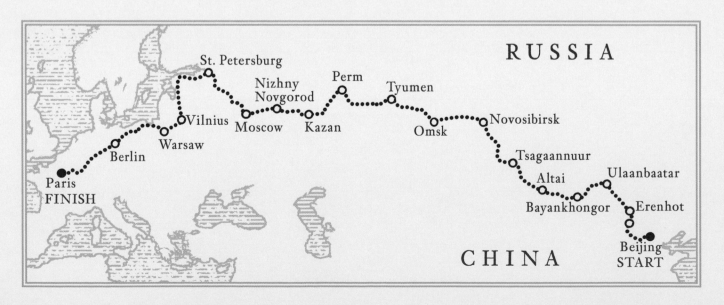

RACE TO THE FINISH

Nearing Europe, roads became better and excitement grew. The Italians were leading the race. A cracked wheel could have cost them victory, but a local carpenter made them a new wheel on the spot. With victory in sight, the prince's team took a detour to have dinner in St. Petersburg! They reached Paris exactly two months after leaving Beijing, giving them an average speed of 6 miles per hour (10 kph)!

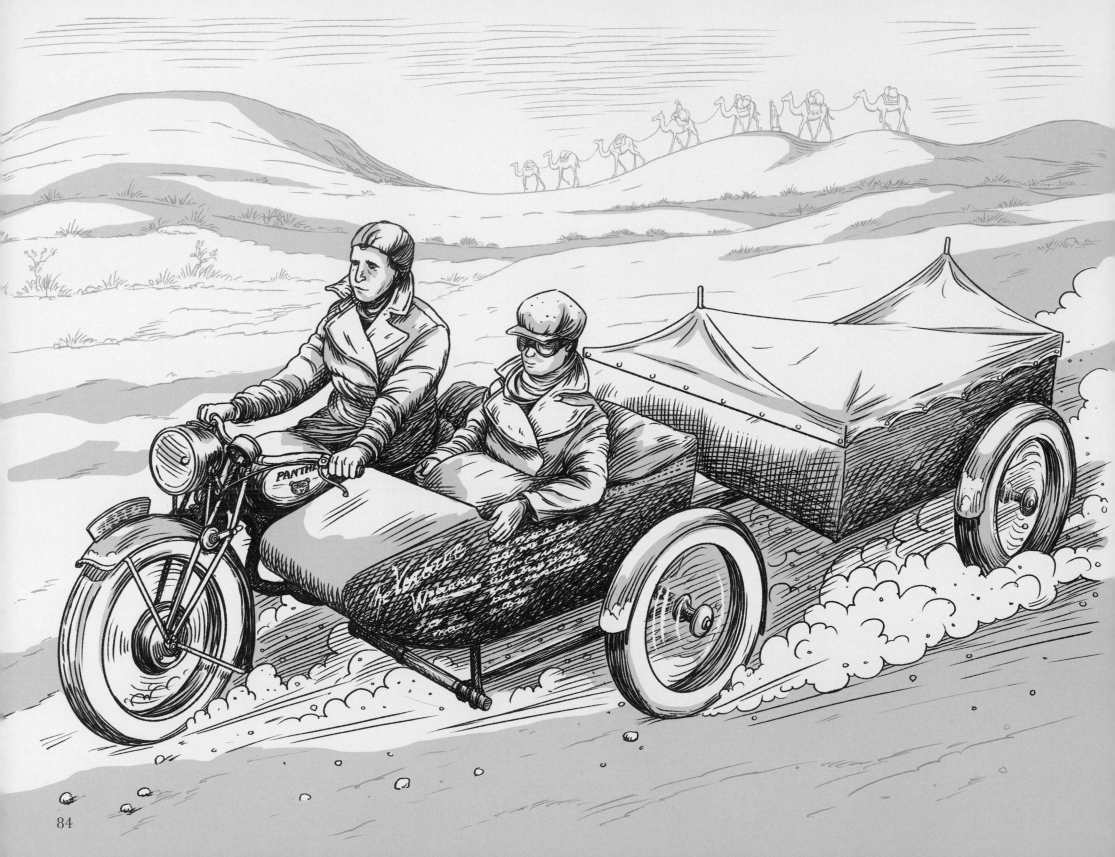

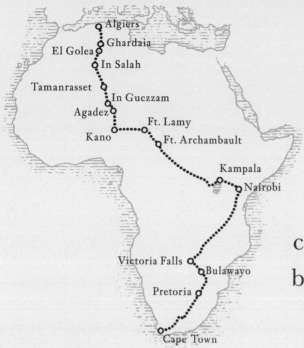

Algiers
Ghardaia
El Golea
In Salah
Tamanrasset
In Guezzam
Agadez
Ft. Lamy
Kano
Ft. Archambault
Kampala
Nairobi
Victoria Falls
Bulawayo
Pretoria
Cape Town

TRAILBLAZERS

Theresa Wallach grew up surrounded by African art and objects collected by her father, and dreamed of traveling in this mysterious continent herself. When she met Florence Blenkiron, the two women became instant friends.

A PAIR OF MOTORCYCLISTS

In the 1930s, it was expected that women would become housewives... an idea that Theresa hated. She did everything she could to avoid this, and went to college to study engineering— almost unheard of for a woman at the time. To her parents' horror, she secretly bought a motorcycle: their determined daughter had chosen her path. At a motorcycle race she bumped into Florence Blenkiron, and they soon formed their grand plan to escape housewifery—a motorcycle expedition across Africa, from north to south!

IN SAHARAN SANDS

The pair set off from the Algerian coast in 1935. Their biggest fears were breakdowns in the desert, lack of water, and local nomads with guns, but local officials became problematic, too, almost barring their way. They broke down often but made running repairs, usually pushing the machine. They befriended locals and spent nights around the campfire with Tuareg and Fulani people. When they suffered total engine failure, it took a month for new parts to be shipped from Yorkshire, and the women acted as mechanics to rebuild their mean machine.

IN SAVANNA AND JUNGLE

Once the desert stage was over, it was swamps, rocks, floods, and wildlife that became their main dangers. They encountered snakes, lions, and gorillas. They had an accident in Tanganyika (now Tanzania) with the only car they'd seen for days, and both vehicles were badly damaged. But they remained positive, and the driver of the car supplied Theresa with the title of the book she would go on to write: *The Rugged Road*. Sadly, the manuscript wasn't published during Theresa's lifetime, but it was finally brought to the public's attention in 2001.

FEARLESS FLIERS

Following the Wright brothers' flight in 1903, airplanes developed rapidly and World War I sped up improvements. Back in peacetime, two American aviators won the hearts of the public with two amazing long-distance flights.

CHARLES LINDBERGH

Born in Detroit but raised on a farm in Minnesota, Charles learned mechanical skills at a young age. He dreamed of flying, and as soon as he was able, he became an airplane stuntman and daredevil. He gained the name Lucky Lindy after surviving four crashes! His name would leap onto the newspaper headlines in 1927 when he flew nonstop across the Atlantic, all on his own. Charles had stayed awake for 20 hours of preparation, so he naturally felt tired during the 33.5-hour flight, and reported seeing the clouds turn into animals and start talking to him!

AMELIA EARHART

Five years later, Amelia Earhart became famous for a transatlantic flight of her own. Her journey into the cockpit was tough, because women weren't expected to fly in those days. But Amelia became the best aviator around of either gender. In 1932, she flew from North America to Northern Ireland. When she landed in a field, a surprised farmer asked, "Have you flown far?" Earhart famously replied, "From America!" Sadly, Amelia's plane disappeared on an around-the-world attempt: the flying ace was missing, presumed dead.

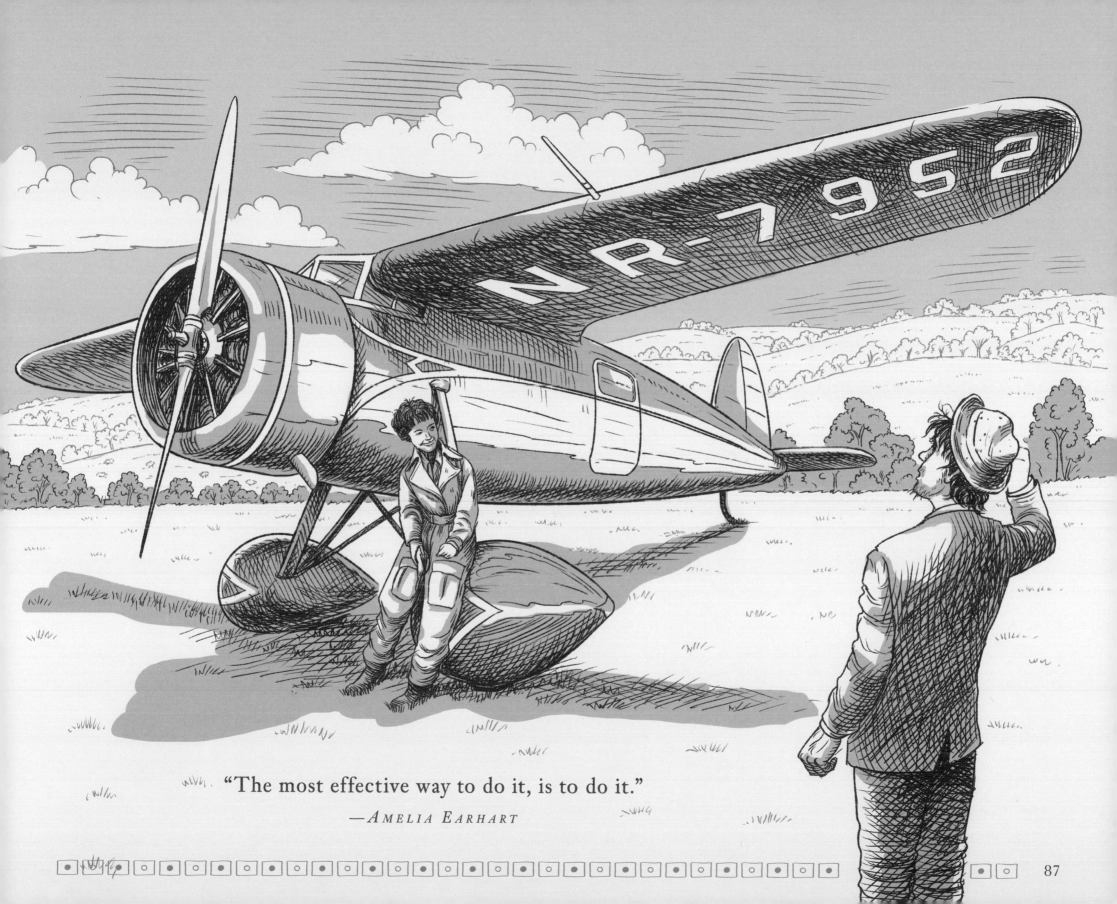

"The most effective way to do it, is to do it."

—AMELIA EARHART

UP *and* DOWN *and* 'ROUND *and* 'ROUND

"Exploration is sport for scientists."
—*AUGUSTE PICCARD*

UP

Auguste Piccard was fascinated by science as a child, so it was no surprise that he became a professor of physics. Extremely tall, with circular spectacles and wild hair, he was a striking figure in the laboratory. But he was an explorer as well as an inventor. He became interested in balloon flight, and designed balloons that could take him higher than humans had ever been before. In 1931, he reached a record height of 9.8 miles (15.8 km), but almost died in the process, as he had to plug a leak with cotton wool and almost ran out of oxygen before drifting wildly over two international borders!

Few families have made as many giant leaps in exploration as the Piccards from Switzerland. Auguste, his son Jacques, and his grandson Bertrand all combined scientific minds with a daredevil spirit and a refusal to be told that something was impossible. They traveled high into the stratosphere, then to the depths of the ocean, then twice around the world.

DOWN

Auguste's son Jacques looked to the depths of the ocean for his big adventure. He designed and built the *Challenger Deep* submersible (underwater vehicle), and in 1960 piloted it to the deepest spot in the sea at the bottom of the Mariana Trench. He heard a clank when the vehicle hit the bottom, and reported seeing a new species of flatfish. However, just like his father, mechanical problems almost cost him his life—he noticed cracks on the *Challenger Deep* and guided it back upward as quickly as he could to prevent a deadly accident.

'ROUND AND 'ROUND

Jacques' son Bertrand was destined to follow in the footsteps of his father and grandfather, but what challenges remained for explorers nearing the 21st century? Well, Bertrand was always interested in flight, and became the first person (with his co-pilot) to fly a balloon nonstop around the globe in 1999. Not satisfied with that record, he became interested in solar-powered vehicles, and together with his co-pilot Andre Borschberg, he became the first person to fly a solar-powered aircraft around the world in 2016. Bertrand has three sons—we look forward to hearing about their adventures in years to come!

MOTORCYCLE DIARIES

In 1952, an Argentinian medical student set off on a motorcycle trip across South America with his friend. The man's name was Ernesto Guevara, but everyone knows him as Che. What started out as a sightseeing trip ended as the beginning of a revolution.

"Let the world change you and you can change the world."

—CHE GUEVARA

BICYCLE DIARIES

Before the big motorcycle trip, Che went on a bicycle ride across Argentina. As he traveled, he noticed that the poorer people were, the more willing they were to help. On his travels, he met his friend Alberto, who spoke about the terrible conditions lived in by people who suffered from leprosy—a disease that left them with disfigured hands and faces. Che became determined to go on a much longer trip to see what life was like across the rest of South America.

TO MINING COUNTRY

Che and Alberto set off in 1952 on a much longer trip, this time on motorcycles. They were determined to speak to hospital patients and prisoners to try to understand the plight of people at the bottom of society. They visited an area famous for its mines in Chile, and saw that the local miners lived in horrible conditions while the foreign owners made huge profits. Che shared conversations with these people by candlelight and even saw some mines for himself firsthand.

LIVING WITH LEPERS

Che took a big interest in the conditions of lepers. In one camp in Peru, lepers were made to live in isolation, despite the disease not being contagious. Che decided to swim across the vast Amazon River and live with the patients, treating them as equals, earning their gratitude.

VIVA LA REVOLUCIÓN!

In total, Che and Alberto traveled more than 5,000 miles (8,000 km), from the bottom to the top of South America. They crossed the Andes, the Atacama Desert, and the Amazon rainforest. But the end of Che's journey was the beginning of another: to help the poor avoid exploitation. He helped the Guatemalans overthrow their government. He is even more famous for his time in Cuba, where he fought for the rights of common people.

OUT OF THIS WORLD

Space was long considered the final frontier, and America and the Soviet Union raced to beat each other to many space "firsts." The Soviets made some of the greatest journeys the world had ever seen, turning science fiction into science fact in the process.

ANIMALS IN SPACE

In 1947, fruit flies became the first creatures sent to space—they zoomed up in a V2 rocket. They were soon followed by a monkey named Albert II in 1949, and then an unnamed mouse in 1950. Two dogs were launched by the Soviets in 1951 and became the first creatures to survive the spaceflight. But the real star of the animal space race was Laika, a stray dog who was sent into orbit in 1957 inside a small spacecraft called *Sputnik 2*. She was a pioneer of space travel.

YURI GAGARIN

Four years after Laika's flight, the Soviet Union launched a manned spaceship. The pilot, Yuri Gagarin, had trained as an airplane pilot and then volunteered for the space program. The *Vostok 1* spacecraft was cramped, but Yuri didn't mind too much, as he'd packed sausages and other snacks to give him energy. Many people thought he would surely die, but he had faith in his success and famously told the ground crew:

"Poyekhali! (Let's go!)"

— *YURI GAGARIN*

VALENTINA TERESHKOVA

In 1963, just two years after Gagarin's spaceflight, Valentina Tereshkova made history as the first woman in space. She worked in a textile factory before her training and enjoyed skydiving as a hobby, making her the perfect candidate for the program. She flew the *Vostok 6* spacecraft and spent more than three days in space, orbiting the Earth 48 times. Years later, she asked to be sent to Mars, even if it was a one-way mission, but this dream was not possible.

TO THE MOON AND BACK

It's incredible to think that man walked on the Moon just eight years after the first human had been into space, and less than twelve years after Laika orbited in the simple *Sputnik* satellite. Incredible, but true. Here's how they did it.

SPACE RACE

Yuri Gagarin's spaceflight in 1961 sparked the Americans to dream of something even bigger. Within days of the Soviet success, President Kennedy asked his space engineers if they could send a man to the Moon and back—"Are we working on it 24 hours a day? If not, why not?" Big dreams needed big money, and the race between the U.S. and the U.S.S.R. was the type of thing that the President would fund—he wanted to win at all costs.

LIFT OFF

The dream soon became a reality, as three men were selected for the *Apollo 11* mission in 1969. Crowds gathered at the launchpad, and record numbers of viewers watched on TV around the world. The rocket successfully completed its flightpath to the Moon, and then released the lunar module with two of the astronauts inside, ready to touch down on the surface of the Moon. Amazingly, the computer that guided them to a safe landing had less computational power than a modern smartphone!

FIRST STEPS

Neil Armstrong had the experience of the first ever moonwalk and reported that he had to think six or seven steps in advance because of the slippery surface, heavy suit, and strange gravity. He collected rock samples and planted an American flag. Buzz Aldrin became the second man to walk on the Moon, and he, too, reported the strangeness but amazingness of the experience —after all, this was a giant leap for mankind!

IN A WORLD OF HIS OWN

And what about Michael Collins, all alone, orbiting the Moon in the command module? He was more isolated than any human being had ever been—for 48 minutes of each orbit, he had no radio contact with his colleagues on the Moon or on Earth. Was he jealous of the men walking on the Moon? Not at all—he was proud of his part in the mission and felt humbled by the vastness of space and mesmerized by the otherworldly views.

"That's one small step for man; one giant leap for mankind."
—NEIL ARMSTRONG

WHERE NEXT?

We've been to the depths of the ocean and to the tips of the mountains, so where are the next set of amazing journeys likely to occur? With advances in technology, the world has become a smaller place, and people have even driven to the North Pole, while others have sailed to the same spot in an icebreaking ship. Traditionalists often try to reenact ancient journeys using ancient technologies, and soloists aim to become the first to reach specific spots without any aid or company.

But one obvious frontier for our species is space, and Mars seems to be the next candidate for human footprints. Who will be wearing the spacesuit, and what will their interplanetary spacecraft look like? Perhaps the first person on Mars will be a reader of this book, while other readers may dream up their own journeys that are just as great and fantastic as the stories already told. Walking is just putting one foot in front of the other; it's the dreaming that is the inspirational bit! Dream big, and enjoy your wanderings.